GARDEN GUIDES

BEDS &
BORDERS

GARDEN GUIDES

BEDS
& BORDERS

LALLIE COX

Illustrations by
ELAINE FRANKS

This is a Parragon Book
This edition published in 2004

Parragon
Queen Street House
4 Queen Street
Bath BA1 1HE

Produced by
Robert Ditchfield Ltd

ISBN 1-40540-152-4

A copy of the British Library Cataloguing in Publication Data is
avaliable from the Library.

Printed in China

ACKNOWLEDGEMENTS

Most of the photographs were taken in the author's garden, Woodpeckers, The Bank, Marlcliff, Bidford-on-Avon.
The publishers would also like to thank the many people and organizations who have allowed photographs to
be taken for this book, including the following:

Acton Beauchamp Roses, Worcester, Barnsley House; Polly Bolton, Nordybank Nurseries, Clee St Margeret;
Burford House, Tenbury Wells; Dinmore Manor; Richard Edwards, Well Cottage, Blakemere; Lance Hattatt,
Arrow Cottage, Weobley; Mr and Mrs James Hepworth, Elton Hall; The Hon Mrs Peter Healing, The Priory,
Kemerton; Hergest Croft Garden; Mrs David Lewis, Ash Farm, Much Birch; Mottisfont Rose Gardens (National
Trust); Mr and Mrs Roger Norman, Marley Bank, Whitbourne; Powis Castle (National Trust); Royal Botanic
Gardens, Kew; RHS Garden, Wisley; Stone House Cottage, Kidderminster; Raymond Treasure, Stockton Bury
Farm, Kimbolton; Mrs David Williams-Thomas, The Manor House, Birlingham.

Photographs of *Origanum* 'Kent Beauty', *Primula vialii, Salix alba vitellina* 'Britzensis', *Tropaeolum speciosum* and
border or foxgloves and penstemons are reproduced by kind permission of Dr. A. Cox.

CONTENTS

Poisonous Plants

In recent years, concern has been voiced about poisonous plants or plants which can cause allergic reactions if touched. The fact is that many plants are poisonous, some in a particular part, others in all their parts. For the sake of safety, it is always, without exception, essential to assume that no part of a plant should be eaten unless it is known, without any doubt whatsoever, that the plant or its part is edible and that it cannot provoke an allergic reaction in the individual person who samples it. It must also be remembered that some plants can cause severe dermatitis, blistering or an allergic reaction if touched, in some individuals and not in others. It is the responsibility of the individual to take all the above into account.

How to Use This Book

Where appropriate, approximate measurements of a plant's height have been given, and also the spread where this is significant, in both metric and imperial measures. The height is the first measurement, as for example 1.2m × 60cm/4 × 2ft. However, both height and spread vary so greatly from garden to garden since they depend on soil, climate and position, that these measurements are offered as guides only. This is especially true of trees and shrubs where ultimate growth can be unpredictable.

The following symbols are also used throughout the book:

    ◖ = thrives best or only in full sun
    ◑ = thrives best or only in part-shade
    ● = succeeds in full shade
    E = evergreen

Where no sun symbol and no reference to sun or shade is made in the text, it can be assumed that the plant tolerates sun or light shade.

Plant Names

For ease of reference this book gives the botanical name under which a plant is most widely listed for the gardener. These names are sometimes changed and in such cases the new name has been included. Common names are given wherever they are in frequent use.

8

BEDS AND BORDERS

TREES AND BULBS will grow happily in grass, but if you want to grow cultivated plants they need to be planted in beds and borders. Here they can be offered the very best conditions in which to grow, free from the competition of weeds. By sympathetically grouping together a diversity of plants a beautiful border can be created.

Ideally the border should be in full or partial sun and sheltered from cold wind. Do not despair if your garden is shaded all day by neighbouring trees or on a windswept hillside. You can have beautiful borders by selecting plants that will thrive in these inhospitable conditions.

THE SHAPE OF YOUR BORDER

Formal geometric beds in the form of straight-sided rectangles and squares or circles are a good choice for a small garden. The formality can be reinforced by arranging the

A harmonious combination of pink dicentra, geranium and thalictrum, mauve nepeta, planted in clumps, drawn together by the ribbon of magenta *Gladiolus byzantinus*.

plants in a repetitive pattern. Alternatively they may be planted in a free informal manner within this formal framework to good effect.

It is more difficult to get a well balanced planting in a bed with natural curves, especially in an island bed. Form has to be created within the planting itself by the use of bold clumps, structural evergreens and architectural plants. Laying a hosepipe on the ground will help you create the shape you want but do not make too many curves. Look at the shape you have created from an upstairs window. Island beds look best in a large garden where there is a view beyond the bed.

If you garden on a hillside you may wish to terrace it with retaining walls to create raised beds.

WHAT TO GROW

Annuals, which flower in their first year from seed and then die, are useful for a bed in its first season where perennial weeds are a problem. Thorough digging can be repeated the following winter.

Bedding plants give an instant garden and can be changed with the seasons. This is a good solution for small beds in small gardens but there is no sense of permanence.

Herbaceous borders planted entirely with perennial plants will be very impressive when flowering exuberantly in summer and early autumn but will be of little interest in winter when the plants are resting. They are best suited to large gardens where they can be sited some distance from the house.

Mixed borders using a medley of trees, shrubs, perennials, annuals, biennials and bulbs can be planned to provide some interest every day of the year. This is the best solution for most gardeners.

The choice of plants is a personal preference but they must suit the soil and climate. Light sandy soils will support a different range of plants to those growing on heavy clay. Soil acidity, measured as the pH, is of importance to some plants: for example rhododendrons and many heathers require an acid soil.

Plants growing well in neighbouring gardens will do equally well for you but you will want to introduce some new ideas. Visit gardens that are open to the public, take a notebook with you and note down plants you like, where they are growing and which plants look good together. Do not be afraid to ask the gardener or the owner about the plants.

Look for plants which have attractive form, good foliage and a long season of interest: plants which produce attractive fruits after flowering or a second crop of flowers.

PREPARING THE SITE

Before any planting can be done the bed needs to be well dug and all perennial weeds removed. If the site is very weedy a herbicide can be used to kill the weeds a few weeks before digging.

On sandy light soils dig in as much compost or manure as you can afford. On heavy clay incorporate grit in addition to these organic bulky manures to improve drainage. If the soil is very badly drained consider making raised beds.

Fish, blood and bone fertilizer applied at planting time will give the plants a good start.

The path leads the way to a seat flanked by twin though different borders of cool colours: mauve nepeta and blue linum.

DESIGNING WITH PLANTS

The aim is to create a harmonious border by marrying good structure with contrasts of colour and texture in flower and foliage.

Flowers are what you first think of, but a border should look good when not in flower. Plants with good form and foliage need to be planned for first.

A sunny border composed of golden kniphofia and coral alstroemeria.

Evergreen shrubs provide a good background to flowers and give solidity to the border. Balance these with flowering shrubs and bold clumps of perennials with architectural merit. Vary the size and shape of these plants contrasting low growing horizontal subjects with rounded forms and the occasional vertical emphasis.

These structural plants are permanent and the space allocated to them needs to accommodate their eventual size. The best way to determine their positions is to plot them on a plan of the border drawn to scale.

Herbaceous plants look best planted in bold clumps and drifts. Although tall plants will generally be planted at the back and short at the front a more interesting picture will be created by bringing the occasional tall plant forward and allowing some short ground-covering plants to flow backwards into the border. Choose flowers of varying form and texture.

As well as grading by size you may wish to grade by colour. Pale colours are easier to blend and harmonize than bright ones. Subtle contrasts of colour and changes of tone can build up to the vivid hues. Flower gardens rarely clash badly but orange-reds need to be kept away from blue-reds. This can be done by separating them with green or silver foliage or pale creamy flowers.

Good foliage is an essential ingredient of a successful border. Green and silver leaves will link the flowering plants and enhance them. Look for contrast in habit, size and texture when choosing foliage. Brightly variegated and red foliage is useful used sparingly.

Good plant associations can lift a border from good to excellent. Try to give every plant the best neighbour you can find for it. Look at associations that please you in other gardens and magazines: you will notice that contrasts of form, texture and colour will have been used. Beware, however, of too much contrast or the planting will appear restless. Calm and stability can be imposed on a border by repeating a good plant at regular intervals to unite the whole.

Allium aflatunense is one of the most ornamental onions, carefully placed against a background of pale pink clematis.

BORDER MAINTENANCE

A newly planted bed will need watering for the first week or so and in dry periods in the first summer.

It is essential to keep on top of the task of weeding because weeds compete with your cultivated plants for water and nutrients as well as looking unsightly.

By removing the dead heads of flowers you will keep the border tidy and encourage the

A bed at the foot of a shady wall with ferns, dicentra and pink trillium.

plant to make new flower buds. Do not dead-head plants that are going to produce decorative seed heads or fruits, such as honesty or rugosa roses.

Perennials will in most cases need to be cut to the ground in late autumn. Mulching with compost or manure every year will improve soil structure and fertility. A boost to growth in spring can be given by top-dressing the beds with a general organic or inorganic fertilizer.

Many perennials spread rapidly into big clumps. They need to be lifted, divided and healthy pieces replanted with fresh compost and fertilizer.

Some plants will need staking, but for ease of maintenance choose those that do not. Bamboo canes and string, hazel twigs and

Penstemon is an invaluable plant which flowers over a long period in summer. This rich, dark cultivar is 'Blackbird'.

patent metal supports all have a place in staking.

Shrubs, roses and clematis will need pruning, but consult a pruning guide as plants differ as to the time and method of pruning.

If you include annuals and biennials these will need to be raised from seed every year.

THE TIME-SCALE OF A BORDER

A border when planted is not like a finished painting. In time, growth will alter the scale of plants. In a mixed border the structural framework of evergreens and deciduous shrubs will take about five years to reach reasonable maturity. They must be given space at planting time to reach this potential. By all means fill the spaces between them with other plants but in the knowledge that some of

The glamorous *Tulipa* 'Black Parrot' thrives at the foot of a hot stony wall.

these will be overwhelmed by the shrubs as they mature.

The planting is not finite. Plants do not always grow as you expect them to, so be prepared to move them around the border the following season. Our taste changes, as does fashion in plants, so always consider replacing a plant that no longer gives you pleasure.

No border is ever perfect but we can have great fun introducing new ideas in our attempt to make it so.

13

1. MIXED BORDERS

Borders for all seasons. The choice of plants is personal but suitability of soil and aspect need to be considered.

The COTTAGE GARDEN

IMAGINE A GARDEN OF SWEET DISORDER having no preconceived plan other than a path to the front door edged with lavender and old-fashioned pinks. The entire garden is treated as a mixed border with a miscellany of shrubs, perennials and bulbs interspersed with vegetables and herbs. This timeless haphazard planting translates well to the garden of a small modern house.

A fine early summer display of 'Shirley' poppies and stately delphiniums in a cottage garden.

◆ *Both these plants are easily raised from seed.*

A cottage border such as this would undoubtedly be crammed with spring-flowering bulbs such as snowdrops, narcissus, tulips and crocus. The perennials are cut down in the autumn and the annuals pulled up once they have shed their seed.

A cottage garden border in summer. Sweet peas climbing on a wig-wam of hazel poles are surrounded by an informal planting of typical cottage garden plants: perennial delphiniums and lupins and annual cornflowers and marigolds. The path is edged with pinks, chives and strawberries. Runner beans, attractive in flower and fruit, would be equally suitable for growing on the poles.

COTTAGE GARDEN PLANTS

LUPINS, DELPHINIUMS AND HOLLYHOCKS – such are the cottager's flowers, underplanted with tulips, anemones, primroses and violets. Around them are self-seeding aquilegias, forget-me-nots, foxgloves and easily grown shrubs such as philadelphus or forsythia with gooseberry and blackcurrant bushes. Roses, clematis, honeysuckle and sweet peas complete the picture.

Daphne mezereum
Deliciously scented flowers before the leaves in early spring. There is a white form. 1.2 × 1.2m/4 × 4ft

Lupins look shabby after flowering. Disguise them by siting a taller, later flowering, plant in front.

Allow some aquilegias to self-seed. Interesting forms and colour variations will occur.

Grow parsley and chives as an edging down the side of the garden path.

Digitalis purpurea
Common foxgloves are red, but pink, white, cream and apricot flowers occur. Biennial. 1.2m × 60cm/ 4 × 2ft

Double forms of the primrose are cottage favourites. They are now obtainable in a variety of colours. 15 × 20cm/6 × 8in

Aquilegia vulgaris 'Nora Barlow' Interesting form of colombine or Granny's bonnet for early summer. 1m × 45cm/3 × 1½ft

Allium schoenoprasum 'Forescate' Pink-flowered form of the common chive. A good edging plant. 30 × 30cm/1 × 1ft

Mentha suaveolens 'Variegata' A culinary mint grown for its attractive summer foliage. 30 × 60cm/1 × 2ft

Rosa 'Tuscany Superb' An old Gallica rose of velvety, dark, blackish crimson, flowering in midsummer. 1 × 1m/3 × 3ft

Paeonia officinalis 'Rubra Plena' An old cottage garden peony flowering in early summer. Good foliage. 60 × 60cm/2 × 2ft

Lupins are early summer perennials in a wide range of colours and easily seed-raised. ○, 1.2m × 60cm/ 4 × 2ft

Alcea rosea Hollyhocks look and grow best in a wall border in full sun. Many colours. 2m × 60cm/6 × 2ft

Philadelphus coronarius Midsummer flowering shrub. Creamy white flowers. Powerful fragrance. 2.4 × 2m/8 × 6ft

Syringa vulgaris 'Alba' White form of common lilac, highly scented flowers in early summer. 3 × 2.4m/10 × 8ft

Delphiniums Large-flowered hybrids for early summer. ○, 2.4 × 1m/8 × 3ft

◆ *The stately spikes require discreet staking.*

HERBACEOUS PERENNIALS

THESE PLANTS ARE THE MAINSTAY OF THE MIXED BORDER from spring until autumn. They die to the ground in winter and re-emerge in spring. They establish quickly, flowering well in their first year. Most are easily propagated by division so plant numbers are soon built up.

Persicaria bistorta **'Superba'** (syn. *Polygonum*) Self-supporting pink spikes for a long season in summer. ○, 60 × 60cm/ 2 × 2ft

Achillea millifolium **'Lilac Beauty'** Flowers from midsummer until autumn. Attractive feathery foliage. ○, 1m × 60cm/3 × 2ft

Digitalis ferruginea A perennial foxglove with slender architectural spikes of an unusual shade. ●, 1m × 30cm/3 × 1ft

Campanula persicifolia Nodding blue or white bells in summer. Will seed about discreetly. ○, 1m × 30cm/ 3 × 1ft

Encourage perennials to flower again by removing dead flower-heads and feeding the plant.

Stake plants early so that by flowering time the stakes will be concealed by foliage.

Many perennials are easily raised from seed sown in early autumn or in the spring.

Penstemon glaber is one of the smaller and hardier penstemons. It will reward you with flowers from early summer until the frosts. Penstemons come in many lovely shades and need a well drained fertile soil in full sun. ○, 60 × 60cm/ 2 × 2ft

◆ *Minimize frost damage by delaying cutting back until late spring. Take easily rooted summer cuttings to replace winter losses.*

A mixed border in early summer. Perennials interlaced with blue forget-me-nots are planted against a back-drop of yellow-leaved shrubs. Deep blue aquilegias and yellow Welsh poppies (*Meconopsis cambrica*) merge prettily together. A white flowered aquilegia with variegated foliage and the bright leaves of *Iris pallida* 'Variegata' make a dramatic splash at the front of the border.

Aquilegia vulgaris The flowers of these long-spurred columbines float like butterflies in early summer. These perennials are very easy to grow from seed. 1m × 45cm/3 × 1½ft

FOLIAGE

An abundance of healthy green foliage will enhance the appearance of flowers. Red, silver and variegated leaves are useful but need to be used with discretion. Look for contrast in size, shape and texture of leaf.

Hedera colchica **'Sulphur Heart'** An excellent ivy to grow up a pole or for ground cover. E, climber to 5m/16ft

Stipa tenuissima A soft textured, fine leaved grass which moves gracefully in the breeze. Plumes of feathery flowers are produced in summer. It fades to buff in autumn. ○, 60 × 45cm/ 2 × 1½ft

Symphytum × uplandicum **'Variegatum'** Stunning cream variegated foliage for shade. Cut down the lilac spikes after they have flowered. Any plain green leaves that develop should be removed. ●, 1m × 60cm/ 3 × 2ft

Euphorbia nicaeensis The neat silver foliage looks good all the year. Greenish yellow flowers in summer. ○, E, 40 × 60cm/1½ × 2ft

Geranium renardii has pretty purple-veined white flowers, but grow it for its lovely textured foliage. ○, 30 × 30cm/1 × 1ft

Alchemilla mollis Downy, soft green, veined leaves. Frothy yellow green flowers. 45 × 45cm/1½ × 1½ft

Hosta sieboldiana grown principally for its big, textured leaves has cool white flowers. 1 × 1.5m/ 3 × 5ft

◆ *Requires moisture and some shade. Beware of slugs.*

FOLIAGE

Alchemilla mollis is a prodigious seeder so remove flowering stems before the seeds ripen.

Many grasses retain their form in winter so delay cutting them down until the spring.

Paulownia is a tree which when young can be cut hard back every spring to produce very large leaves.

23

EVERGREEN SHRUBS

EVERGREEN SHRUBS GIVE A PERMANENT STRUCTURE to a border at all seasons and provide an excellent background for flowering plants. Conifers, particularly those of fastigiate or prostrate habit, can be useful but restrict yourself to one or two. Evergreens such as yew, box and holly can be tightly clipped to impose a year-round formality upon the border.

Euonymus fortunei 'Silver Queen' Creamy white variegation. 1 × 1.5m/3 × 5ft

Brachyglottis 'Sunshine' (syn. *Senecio*) Silver leaved shrub for a sunny well-drained spot. Yellow flowers. ◯, 1.2 × 2m/4 × 6ft

◆ *A blue clematis looks good growing through this shrub.*

Hebe rakaiensis This apple-green rounded shrub is outstanding in the dull days of winter ◯, 1 × 1.2m/ 3 × 4ft

Eucalyptus gunnii grown as a shrub by pruning annually in late spring.

EVERGREEN SHRUBS

The very dark green of **Taxus baccata**, the common yew, gives a permanency to this border and makes an excellent background for the white-flowering shrub and bright perennials.

◆ *The narrowly upright Irish yew,* Taxus baccata *'Fastigiata', is useful for imposing formality on a border.*

Santolina or **'Cotton Lavender'** is an ideal evergreen shrub to clip tightly into balls for formal foliage effect.

Ilex aquifolium **'Ferox Argentea'** A variegated holly, unique in having prickles over the entire leaf surface. No berries. 2.4 × 2.4m/8 × 8ft

A clipped spiral of **Buxus sempervirens**, the common box, planted in a pot adds interest to a border.

FLOWERING SHRUBS

Camellia 'Water Lily'
Flowers in early spring.
Acid or neutral soil and
shade from morning sun
essential. ◑, E, 3 × 2.4m/
10 × 8ft

Space flowering shrubs far
enough apart for them to
achieve their ultimate
spread without
encroachment.

If a spring-flowering
ceanothus needs cutting
back, do this immediately it
has finished flowering.

Buddleja davidii should be
pruned hard in late winter.
Prune *B. crispa* lightly in
late spring.

Ceanothus 'Puget Blue'
Neat-textured evergreen
foliage. Blue flowers in
early summer. ○, E, 1.5 ×
2.4m/5 × 8ft

**Daphne × burkwoodii
'Somerset'** Variegated,
sweetly scented, white-
throated pink flowers in
spring. ○, 1.5 × 1m/5 × 3ft

Buddleja crispa A summer-
long succession of orange-
throated lilac flowers.
Beautiful felted leaves. ○,
2.4 × 2.4m/8 × 8ft

Choisya ternata Glossy
green leaves compliment
the scented white flowers of
Mexican orange blossom.
○, E, 2 × 2m/6 × 6ft

**Chaenomeles speciosa
'Nivalis' (Flowering
quince)** Flowers over a long
period in early spring.
1.5 × 1.5m/5 × 5ft

**Rosmarinus officinalis
(Rosemary)** An aromatic
small shrub, flowering in
spring/early summer ○, E,
1 × 1m/3 × 3ft

**Potentilla fruticosa
'Katherine Dykes'** Flowers
late spring until autumn.
Good drainage and full sun.
○, 60cm × 1m/2 × 3ft

FLAMBOYANT FLOWERING SHRUBS often have a very short flowering period. When choosing them always consider how they will look when not in flower: elegance of habit and attractive foliage are important. Include some with scent to fill your garden with perfume.

Abutilon × *suntense* Flowers in early summer. Appreciates a warm and sheltered position. ○, 4 × 3m/13 × 10ft

◆ *This is a beautiful shrub but it is not fully hardy.*

Indigofera heterantha Prettily divided leaves. Mauve-pink flowers all summer. ○, 3 × 3m/ 10 × 10ft

Hydrangea villosa The velvety leaves of this shrub set of the lace-cap flowers to perfection. ●, 2.4 × 2m/ 8 × 6ft

Magnolia × *loebneri* **'Leonard Messel'** A narrow elegant tree 4.5 × 2.4m/15 × 8ft

◆ *Winter attraction of branch pattern and buds.*

ROSES

OLD ROSES BLOOM EFFUSIVELY, looking and smelling wonderful in early summer. Look also for roses with a longer or repeated flowering period and those with other attributes such as good foliage, nice hips or interesting thorns. A climbing rose on a wall or up a pole will add another dimension.

If pruned hard *Rosa glauca* will produce no flowers or hips but abundant fresh foliage.

Dead-head roses throughout the season to encourage more flowers – apart from varieties with good hips.

'Stanwell Perpetual' is seldom without a sweetly scented flower from early summer until late autumn. 1.5 × 1.5m/5 × 5ft

'Cécile Brunner' has perfectly shaped tiny pink buds on a sparse bush. Also available as a climbing rose. 75 × 60cm/2½ × 2ft

'Nevada' A large shrub rose with a spectacular early-summer flowering. A few flowers in autumn. 2.4 × 2.4m/8 × 8ft

'Iceberg' The climbing form of this popular cluster rose makes an excellent pillar rose climbing to 2.4m/8ft.

An association of roses with a complementary planting of perennials. *Rosa glauca*, a vigorous shrub with handsome purple-grey foliage, has small single cerise flowers (not shown) followed by red autumnal hips. The double pink, fragrant flowers of **'Mary Rose'** are produced throughout the rose season on a sturdy bush. *Geranium endressii* and *Viola cornuta* complete the picture.

FLOWERS *to plant* with ROSES

FLOWERS IN SHADES OF PINK, PURPLE, LILAC, WHITE AND CREAMY YELLOW associate well with the pinks, whites and crimsons of the old roses. Campanulas, violas and hardy geraniums are excellent companion plants. The brighter tones of modern roses are best complemented by using flowers of similar but softer hues, toned down with cool silver and green foliage.

Clematis viticella '**Purpurea Plena Elegans**' A late-flowering clematis, lovely growing through a pink rose. Climber to 2.4m/8ft

If *Viola cornuta* gets straggly in mid-season, revive it by cutting it right down.

When *Rosa complicata* has finished flowering, prune out all stems that have flowered.

Prune viticella varieties of clematis almost to the ground in late autumn or early spring.

A harmonious mixed border of roses and other plants. *Rosa complicata*, which has large bright-pink single flowers with white and yellow centres, is here associated with white foxgloves and the blue form of *Campanula persicifolia*, the peach-leaved bell flower.

Viola cornuta An easy viola flowering prodigiously. White, lilac and deep violet forms available. E, 30 × 60cm/1 × 2ft

FLOWERS *to plant with* ROSES

Allium aflatunense A stately ornamental onion to associate with the Burnet roses of early summer. 1.2m × 30cm/4 × 1ft

***Geranium* 'Johnson's Blue'** Intense lavender-blue flowers are lovely planted with pale yellow roses. 30 × 60cm/1 × 2ft

***Artemisia absinthium* 'Lambrook Silver'** Grown for its silky, silver foliage. Highly aromatic. ○, E, 60 × 60cm/2 × 2ft

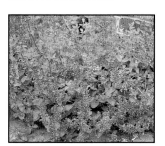

Nepeta racemosa An excellent edging plant for rose beds. Catmint flowers throughout the season. ○, 45 × 45cm/1½ × 1½ft

***Salvia officinalis* 'Purpurascens'** The purple-leaved form of the shrubby culinary sage. ○, E, 60cm × 1m/2 × 3ft

Stachys byzantina (syn. *S. lanata*, Lamb's ears) forms a carpet of weed-suppressing, woolly, silver leaves. ○, E, 45 × 30cm/1½ × 1ft

Sisyrinchium striatum Iris-like foliage and spikes of creamy yellow flowers which close in late afternoon. E, 60 × 30cm/2 × 1ft

***Geranium* × *riversleaianum* 'Mavis Simpson'** A hybrid geranium which flowers profusely all summer long. ○, 30cm × 1m/1 × 3ft

Geranium sanguineum* var. *striatum A lovely pink form of the bloody cranesbill, flowering for many weeks. ○, 30 × 45cm/1 × 1½ft

◆ *More flowers are induced by cutting back mid-season.*

VERY SMALL BEDS

IT IS OFTEN BEST to treat a very small bed in a formal manner and confine the planting to neat low growing plants with attractive foliage: an edging of box always looks good. Seasonal interest can be introduced with bulbs and bedding plants. In this way changes can be made each year.

Two small square beds are edged with box which is clipped into balls at each corner. A standard 'lollipop' *Euonymus fortunei* 'Emerald 'n' Gold' is planted in the centre. These evergreen shrubs are attractive the year round. This basic planting is enlivened by using seasonal bedding. Seen here with **tulip 'West Point'** and **forget-me-nots**, it could have red pelargoniums in summer.

This bed is also box-edged but here the box is clipped tightly into balls to frame a specimen plant of **Yucca gloriosa 'Variegata'**.

◆ *Box is easily grown from cuttings so it need not be expensive if you are patient.*

By treating two or more beds identically a sense of unity and permanence is bestowed upon the garden.

Bold plants such as the echeverias, seen here bedded with airy nemesia, make an impact.

◆ *Echeverias are not hardy and need winter protection.*

A WINTER BORDER

A VERY SATISFYING BORDER can be made with winter-flowering shrubs, trees with interesting bark, evergreens, early-flowering perennials and bulbs. Ideally the border should be visible from the house with the low winter sun illuminating it. Alternatively site it by a path or entrance-drive where you walk, as many winter flowers are highly scented.

Jasminum nudiflorum The cheerful winter jasmine has yellow flowers on green stems. It flowers best grown on a wall for support and protection. Climbing to 2m/6ft.

Acer griseum (**Paper-bark maple**) Small tree with cinnamon-brown peeling bark. Glows in winter sunshine. 8 × 6m/26 × 20ft

Salix alba vitellina '**Britzensis**' A willow with glowing orange-red bark on coppiced stems. 1.5 × 1.5m/5 × 5ft

Viburnum × bodnantense '**Dawn**' Pink, scented flowers adorn the naked branches for many weeks. 3 × 2m/10 × 6ft

Hamamelis × intermedia A witch-hazel with fragrant yellow spidery flowers on bare branches. Acid soil, 2.4 × 3m/8 × 10ft

Viburnum tinus A handsome evergreen. White flowers from pink buds in late winter. E, 2.4 × 2.4m/ 8 × 8ft

Iris unguicularis The Algerian iris has scented flowers throughout the winter. Needs hot dry spot. ○, E, 60 × 30cm/2 × 1ft

Cyclamen coum Brave little pink or white flowers for many weeks which defy the frost. 10 × 15cm/4 × 6in

Galanthus nivalis Aptly named the harbingers of spring, snowdrops are easy to grow, appreciating some shade. 15 × 15cm/6 × 6in

A WINTER BORDER

Helleborus foetidus 'Wester Flisk' Bunches of maroon edged, green flowers over evergreen foliage. E, 45 × 45cm/1½ × 1½ft

Bergenia purpurascens Bold, shiny, green leaves change to burnished red in cold weather. E, 30 × 45cm/ 1 × 1½ft

Heathers and conifers make excellent bed-fellows. Conifers grown for their varying forms and colour changes are enlivened by the heathers in late winter.

◆ *Red, pink or white, winter-flowering heather,* Erica carnea, *will tolerate alkaline soil.*

2. SUNNY BEDS AND BORDERS

Memories of high summer – hot baked earth with silver-foliaged, aromatic plants revelling in these hard conditions.

HOT, DRY BORDERS

ON A SANDY OR STONY SOIL, rain drains through very quickly taking nutrients with it. If the garden is on a slope facing the sun it will be very dry indeed. However, this is exactly what some plants demand: many silver-leaved plants will only thrive in such conditions.

The plants in this very hot, dry, sunny spot have been well-chosen and are obviously thriving. *Cistus* 'Peggy Sammons', penstemon and a graceful dierama are enhanced by silver-leaved shrubs.

◆ *The pots contain purple sage, lavender and a tender aeonium.*

HOT, DRY BORDERS

Cistus purpureus An aromatic evergreen shrub which covers itself with bloom in early summer. ◯, E, 1.2 × 1m/4 × 3ft

Convolvulus sabatius displays a succession of lavender-blue flowers on trailing stems all summer long. This convolvulus is not invasive. ◯, 15 × 45cm/6in × 1½ft

◆ *In cold districts grow in a pot and overwinter under glass.*

Helianthemum 'Annabel' A lovely double form of rock rose with a long flowering season. ◯, E, 30 × 45cm/ 1 × 1½ft

◆ *Cut back hard when flowering has finished.*

Yucca gloriosa 'Variegata' An architectural plant with evergreen leaves. E, 1.2 × 1m/4 × 3ft

◆ *Dramatic spikes of white flowers in late summer.*

The seat invites you to bide awhile amongst the fragrant **Madonna lilies (*Lilium candidum*)**. The scented climbing rose **'Golden Showers'** and *Solanum crispum* **'Glasnevin'** flower for many weeks.

A SUNNY WALL

THE BORDER AT THE FOOT OF A SUNNY WALL will be very hot on a summer afternoon. Choose plants that enjoy a baking. In winter this will be the warmest spot particularly if the wall is that of a house. Here is an opportunity to try something a little tender that cannot be grown in the open.

Abutilon megapotamicum A graceful wall shrub in flower for the entire summer.
○, 3 × 3m/10 × 10ft

◆ *This is a tender plant but worth trying in a sunny, sheltered corner.*

Agapanthus **Headbourne Hybrids** A very hardy strain of the blue African lily.
○, 60 × 45cm/2 × 1½ft

41

GRAVEL BORDERS

A GRAVEL BORDER adjacent to a terrace or drive makes an interesting and harmonious link to a lawn. Plants that need good drainage will thrive in this environment. Site in full sun, excavate 15–20cm/6–8in of soil and replace with small limestone chippings.

Dianthus **'Rose de Mai'** An old-fashioned pink of spreading habit with an abundance of flower. ○, E, 20 × 45cm/8in × 1½ft

Erigeron karvinskianus A fascinating little daisy flower. The flowers open white and turn pink with age. ○, 15 × 30cm/6in × 1ft

◆ *This will seed about in a delightful way.*

Erinus alpinus A tiny plant which seeds happily around in gravel. Flowers red, mauve, pink or white ○, E, 7.5 × 7.5cm/3 × 3in

A gravel terrace bed in early summer with pinks, campanulas, diascias and a carpet of pink and white *Thymus serpyllum*. *Erigeron karvinskianus* will be covered with little daisies until the autumn.

◆ *The pot is planted with sempervivums (houseleeks). The evergreen rosettes change colour with the seasons.*

GRAVEL BORDERS

***Origanum* 'Kent Beauty'**
Unusual green and purple papery bracts on trailing stems. Flowers dry well. ○, 15 × 30cm/6in × 1ft

Calamintha nepeta Dainty ice-blue flowers produced usefully in late summer. Aromatic foliage. 45 × 60cm/18 × 24in

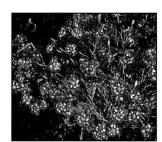

***Dianthus* 'Waithman's Beauty'** A distinctly marked, single, old-fashioned pink; it revels in a hot gravelly site. E, 15 × 23cm/6 × 9in

***Phlox subulata* 'Betty'** A cushion of fine leaves smothered with flowers in early summer. ○, E, 10 × 30cm/4in × 1ft

***Armeria maritima* (Thrift)** From a mat of grass-like leaves arise little stiff-stemmed, round flowers. ○, E, 10 × 20cm/4 × 8in

Campanula poscharskyana A spreading carpeter for gravel but not for small beds. 15cm/6in × indefinite

***Linum* 'Gemmell's Hybrid'** Very bright yellow flowers over a neat semi-evergreen dome. ○, E, 15 × 20cm/ 6 × 8in

Pulsatilla vulgaris The flowers of the Pasque flower are followed by beautiful feathery seed heads. ○, 30 × 30cm/1 × 1ft

◆ *There are lovely white, red, pink and pale lavender forms.*

Cut back pinks (dianthus), phlox, aubrieta and alyssum immediately after flowering. New neat foliage grows quickly.

Take cuttings of pinks to replace existing plants as they become leggy and shabby with age.

Do not dead-head pulsatillas or you will miss the lovely seed heads they have.

***Diascia* 'Ruby Field'** One of the hardiest of the diascias. A mat of heart-shaped green leaves. 15 × 20cm/6 × 8in

RAISED BEDS

Gentiana sino-ornata An autumn-flowering gentian demanding moist, acid soil in sun. 7.5 × 23cm/3 × 9in

Delosperma nubigenum A rarely grown plant with tender-looking green leaves. Surprisingly hardy. ○, E, 2.5 × 30cm/1in × 1ft

Euphorbia myrsinites drapes itself over the edge of a raised bed. Attractive at all seasons. ○, E, 15 × 60cm/6in × 2ft

Ramonda myconi is an ideal plant for the shady side of a peat-block wall. ●, E, 7.5 × 15cm/3 × 6in

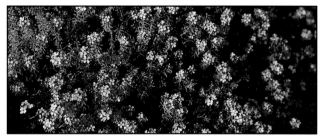

Aethionema 'Warley Rose' A neat little semi-evergreen shrub covered in pink flowers in early summer. ○, 15 × 23cm/6 × 9in

◆ *Take cuttings to ensure replacement for this short-lived plant.*

On chalk, make raised beds for lime-hating plants with peat-block walls and ericaceous compost.

Gardening can be enjoyed from a wheel-chair using narrow raised beds with a foot recess.

Crepis incana Pink dandelion flowers are seen at their best in a raised bed. ○, 20 × 45cm/8in × 1½ft

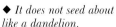

◆ *It does not seed about like a dandelion.*

Sempervivum (Houseleek) Evergreen fleshy rosettes look at home in the crevices of a sunny stone wall.

A BORDER ON TOP OF A TERRACED WALL in a sloping garden, or a raised island bed in an otherwise flat garden adds another dimension in design. Small alpine plants are better appreciated nearer the eye and can be provided with the soil and conditions appropriate to their special needs.

RAISED BEDS

A raised bed made with railway sleepers. *Erysimum* 'Bowles Mauve', helianthemums, saxifrages, pinks and the strikingly variegated *Sisyrinchium striatum* 'Aunt May' jostle happily together.

◆ *All sorts of materials can be used to build retaining walls. Brick and stone are traditional.*

3. SHADY BEDS

A placid oasis of green shade. Hostas, ferns and white flowers make a place to linger long on a hot afternoon.

A SHADY WALL

Jasminum nudiflorum (Winter jasmine), will grow and flower very well against a shady wall.

Sarcococca (Sweet box) is a neat evergreen shade-loving shrub with highly scented winter flowers.

A BORDER AGAINST THE SHADY WALL of a house may need watering occasionally in a dry summer. It is an ideal sheltered spot for plants that like deep shade. The filigree green leaves of ferns and white flowers look particularly good in this situation.

Arum italicum italicum A spectacular foliage plant for winter. Summer-dormant. ●, 25 × 20cm/ 10 × 8in

◆ *These elegant leaves last well in water when picked.*

The climbing **Hydrangea anomala** ssp. **petiolaris** flowers in early summer and reveals its interesting bark and habit in winter. The huge, shiny, tropical-looking leaves of **Fatsia japonica** belie the hardiness of this evergreen shrub. Hostas are at their happiest in shade and ferns revel in such conditions. A dainty form of the lady fern contrasts with the more robust evergreen soft shield fern. A little variegated strawberry weaves about the border.

PLANTING *under* TREES

FEW PLANTS WILL THRIVE in the dense, dry shade of large mature trees but ivy in its many forms grows well to form a dense attractive ground-cover. Smaller deciduous garden trees allow more adventurous planting in their lighter shade. Violets, hellebores and many of the small spring bulbs do well, flowering as they do before the trees come into leaf.

Polygonatum × hybridum
Solomon's seal has elegant curving stems from which hang little white bell-shaped flowers.
1m × 45cm/3 × 1½ft

Watch out for cut-worm caterpillars on the foliage of Solomon's seal after flowering.

Plants will require watering regularly until well established after which they will be self-sufficient.

Cyclamen hederifolium
Winter-hardy, marbled, ivy-shaped leaves follow the tiny flowers of autumn.
10 × 20cm/4 × 8in

Lamium maculatum album
This white-flowered, variegated dead-nettle quickly spreads. 15 × 60cm/6in × 2ft

Euphorbia amygdaloides var. **robbiae** A tough plant to flower well in the deepest and driest shade. E, 60 × 60cm/2 × 2ft

Smilacina racemosa Fluffy white flower spikes at the end of graceful arching stems. Splendid foliage.
75 × 75cm/2½ × 2½ft

◆ *Smilacina grows best in acid soil but will tolerate lime.*

Anemone nemerosa 'Robinsoniana' A cool lavender-blue wood-anemone flowering in late spring. Naturalizes well. 15 × 30cm/6in × 1ft

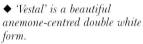

◆ *'Vestal' is a beautiful anemone-centred double white form.*

Lilium martagon var. *album* The easily grown white form of Turk's cap lily. 1.2m × 30cm/4 × 1ft

Iris foetidissima Large seed pods on the Gladwin iris open to reveal bright orange seeds in winter. E, 45 × 60cm/1½ × 2ft

Convallaria majalis Lily-of-the-valley grown for its delicious scent in spring. 20 × 20cm/8 × 8in

◆ *Lovely to pick for the house.*

Symphytum 'Hidcote Blue' A vigorous colonizing comfrey suited to use as ground-cover. 45 × 60cm/ 1½ × 2ft

Dicentra 'Spring Morning' flowers from spring well into summer. Dainty fern-like foliage. 45 × 45cm/ 1½ × 1½ft

Ferns with their lacy foliage make sympathetic companions for all these shade lovers.

Lily-of-the-valley is difficult to eradicate once established, so plant in the right place!

51

MOIST BEDS *in* SEMI-SHADE

MOIST SHADE IS A RARE COMMODITY but at the bottom of a slope on heavy soil or alongside a natural stream or pond you may have it. It can be created artificially with a porous hose laid on or below the surface connected to a water supply. There are many beautiful plants that revel in these conditions, as do weeds!

Erythronium **'Pagoda'** A summer-dormant, spring-flowering tuberous plant. Pale yellow, reflexed, lily-like flowers over glossy foliage. 30 × 20cm/1ft × 8in

If you want to move erythroniums, wait until late summer when they are dormant.

Good plant associations often occur naturally when you plant subjects with similar cultural requirements together.

Corydalis flexuosa may become dormant if dry, but will shoot again as conditions improve.

Primula pulverulenta The flowers are arranged in tiers around the stem, hence the colloquial name of candelabra primula. Shades of dark pink, pink and white harmonize beautifully. 60 × 45cm/2 × 1ft

Primula vialii A unique primula with tightly packed spikes of purple and red. 30 × 20cm/1ft × 8in

Dodecatheon meadia f. **album** A hardy little shooting star with pendant flowers having reflexed petals. 20 × 15cm/8 × 6in

Corydalis flexuosa 'Père David' Dainty fern-like foliage above which dance clear blue spurred flowers. 30 × 30cm/1 × 1ft

Hyacinthoides non-scripta A patch of bluebells will scent the air in early summer. 30 × 10cm/1ft × 4in

Brunnera macrophylla pulmonarioides Forget-me-not flowers over bold green foliage. 45 × 60cm/1½ × 2ft

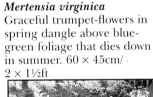

Mertensia virginica Graceful trumpet-flowers in spring dangle above blue-green foliage that dies down in summer. 60 × 45cm/ 2 × 1½ft

Trollius europaeus Incurved globe flowers of cool lemon yellow over good foliage for early summer. 60 × 45cm/ 2 × 1½ft

Carex elata 'Aurea' Bowles' golden sedge needs some sun for brightest coloured foliage. 60 × 60cm/2 × 2ft

The feathery flowers and foliage of astilbe are the perfect foil for the bold-leaved hosta.

◆ *Plants requiring similar conditions frequently look good together.*

Astrantia major has flowers like little green, white and pink Victorian posies. 60 × 45cm/2 × 1½ft

4. PLANTER'S PALETTE

*Plant a perfect picture by blending
subtle tones of flower and foliage and
providing drama with brighter and
contrasting hues.*

A border of pink and lilac flowers looks charming in the soft light of late summer and autumn. This group of late-flowering perennials will be in bloom for many weeks. *Anemone* **'September Charm'** with its simple, pink flowers and the elegant bright lavender-blue spikes of *Perovskia atriplicifolia* are complemented by the filigree silver leaves of *Artemisia* **'Powis Castle'**. Cyclamen and low-growing asters are in the foreground.

AFTER THE SHARP GREENS AND YELLOWS OF SPRING the pale pinks, mauves and blues of early summer create a peaceful, harmonious interlude. The planting can be enlivened with accents of a darker hue such as purple or magenta. The pastels themselves will appear deeper if silver foliage and a few white flowers are included.

PASTELS

Hardy chrysanthemums are ideal plants for the autumn border. Try *Dendranthema* 'Clara Curtis', a single pink.

Kolkwitzia amabilis Pink, yellow-centred flowers smother the beauty bush in early summer. ○, 3 × 3m/ 10 × 10ft

Lavatera 'Barnsley' A fast-growing, short-lived shrub. It flowers continuously throughout the summer. ○, 2 × 1.2m/6 × 4ft

Phlox carolina 'Bill Baker' A clump-forming, early summer flowering, dwarf phlox. 30 × 30cm/1 × 1ft

◆ *This plant will grow in sun or part shade.*

Aster × frikartii A mildew-free Michaelmas daisy flowering from midsummer until autumn. ○, 75 × 60cm/2½ × 2ft

Geranium pratense 'Mrs Kendall Clark' An attractive, pale form of the meadow cranesbill. 75 × 45cm/2½ × 1½ft

Bright Yellows

Lilium 'King Pete' An easily grown hybrid lily. All lilies require good drainage. 60 × 20cm/2ft × 8in

Remove the insignificant flowers of *Valeriana phu* 'Aurea' because any seedlings will have green foliage.

The bright yellow daisies of helenium, heliopsis and inula are good for late summer borders.

Yellow variegated forms of holly or *Euonymus fortunei* have year-round bright foliage.

Euphorbia polychroma bursts into flower in late spring with a long-lasting display of yellow and green bracts. 45 × 60cm/1½ × 2ft

◆ *Forget-me-nots (myosotis) are a lovely combination with this euphorbia.*

Genista hispanica forms a perfectly domed, very prickly green bush. This Spanish gorse covers itself profusely with flowers in early summer. ○, 75cm × 1.2m/2½ × 4ft

Narcissus 'Tête-à-Tête' One of the best little cyclamineus hybrids for early spring. Buttercup-yellow trumpets, often two to a stem. Increases rapidly to make a good clump. 20 × 15cm/ 8 × 6in

◆ *'Tête-à-Tête' is ideal for a raised bed or rock garden. Try it with Crocus chrysanthus 'Blue Pearl'.*

YELLOW IS CHEERFUL AND ATTRACTS ATTENTION. It is enhanced by good green foliage and a few white flowers. The bright shades of yellow harmonise with the hot oranges and orange-reds of late summer to make a very bright border. Year-long interest can be achieved by planting shrubs with yellow or variegated leaves.

BRIGHT YELLOWS

Iris pallida **'Variegata'** retains the beauty of its leaves throughout the summer. ○, 45 × 30cm/ 1½ × 1ft

Valeriana phu **'Aurea'** Eye-catching bright yellow leaves for early spring. ○, 20 × 30cm/8in × 1ft

Euonymus **'Emerald 'n' Gold'** and *Cedrus deodara* **'Golden Horizon'** provide year-long colour and form. A cut-leaved, golden elder adds summer interest.

◆ *Annual poached-egg plant* (Limnanthes douglasii) *and perennial* Corydalis lutea *complete the picture.*

59

PALE YELLOWS

LUMINOUS PALE YELLOWS are useful for softening a bright scheme and show up well at dusk. A border of pale yellow complemented by shades of pale lilac is very restful. It can be made more exciting by strengthening the lilac shades to purple or magenta.

Phygelius aequalis **'Yellow Trumpet'** A long-flowering summer shrub best planted against a sunny wall. ○, 1.2 × 1.2m/4 × 4ft

Tulipa **'Fringed Elegance'** A fine tulip with a crystal-like fringe. ○, 40 × 20cm/ 1½ft × 8in

Anthemis tinctoria **'Alba'** A pale, creamy form of this floriferous perennial. Cut down after flowering. ○, 75 × 75cm/2½ × 2½ft

Primula vulgaris A double form of the common primrose and a favourite flower for spring. 15 × 20cm/6 × 8in

A successful, cool looking border using green and silver foliage and contrasting textures in flower and leaf. Cream and pale yellow flowers are enhanced by a touch of contrasting purple.

Rosa **'The Pilgrim'** A
modern English rose with
flat petal-packed blooms
like the old gallicas.
1 × 1m/3 × 3ft

A pleasing association of pale yellow and
lilac flowers: ***Alcea rugosa*** (a perennial
hollyhock), ***Penstemon*** **'Alice Hindley'**
and ***Clematis*** **'Perle d'Azur'** of slightly
darker hue, are good companions.

◆ *These shades can also be combined
in a spring border using narcissus,
crocus and tulips.*

Kniphofia **'Little Maid'** A
dainty little red hot poker
that is not red! Ideal for a
small garden. Creamy
yellow spikes rise above
grassy foliage. 60 × 45cm/
2 × 1½ft

◆ *Lilac-blue* Aster
thomsonii *'Nanus' is a
good companion for this
late-flowering kniphofia.*

The silvery artemisias
associate well with pale
yellow flowers. All need sun
and good drainage.

It is wise to give kniphofias
a little winter protection
with a mulch of straw.

'Maggie Mott' is an easily
grown viola of clear violet
to associate with these
yellows.

HOT REDS

BRIGHT RED IS EYE-CATCHING and appears to bring the border nearer to the viewer. In a small garden this can make the garden itself feel smaller. Planted with bright green foliage the red will seem even brighter. A more subtle effect is achieved by using harmonizing foliage in tones of brown, black and purple.

Dahlia **'Bishop of Llandaff'** The bright flowers are in perfect harmony with the dark bronze foliage.
75 × 45cm/2½ × 1½ft

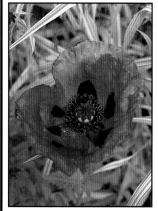

Papaver orientale The oriental poppy of early summer. Avoid seedlings by removing seed heads.
1m × 60cm/3 × 2ft

Rosa moyesii Grow this large species rose for its avalanche of red flask-shaped hips. 4 × 3m/ 13 × 10ft

Tulipa **'Apeldoorn'** A vigorous, very hardy tulip of eye-dazzling red. Nice with cream wallflowers.
60 × 20cm/2ft × 8in

Crocosmia **'Lucifer'** A magnificent tall crocosmia whose sword-like leaves retain their good looks throughout the summer.
1.2m × 30cm/4 × 1ft

◆ *Divide this vigorous plant in spring if it becomes congested.*

Helianthemum **'Supreme'** is one of several good rock roses which provide brilliant pools of colour in summer. For well-drained soil. ○, E, 15 × 45cm/6in × 1½ft

Cordyline australis 'Purpurea' A temporary tender addition to a border for the summer. ○, E, 1m × 60cm/3 × 2ft

Cotinus coggygria 'Royal Purple' This smoke bush is a lovely background shrub for any border. 4 × 4m/ 13 × 13ft

Phormium tenax 'Purpureum' (New Zealand flax) In a sheltered spot this plant will look smart. ○, E, 1.5 × 1.2m/5 × 4ft

HOT REDS

Dahlias need lifting in autumn and storing almost dry in frost-free conditions.

***

Cordylines look well placed in the border still in their pots, which give added height.

Penstemon 'Red Knight' Encourage repeat flowering by cutting out stems that have finished flowering. ○, E, 75 × 45cm/2½ × 1½ft

Euphorbia dulcis 'Chameleon' Brownish purple leaves of summer turn orange-red in autumn. 40 × 40cm/16 × 16in

A background of tall purple-leaved shrubs against which are displayed the scintillating reds of *Lobelia cardinalis*, dahlias and annual tobacco plants.

◆ *The red flowers and foliage are enhanced by the surrounding greens.*

COOL WHITES

WHITE FLOWERS AND GREEN FOLIAGE look sophisticated and are particularly good in the formal planting of geometric beds. White shows up well in a shady corner and in the evening. A large border planted entirely in white needs a dash of one other colour to enliven it: soft apricot or pale blue works well.

Campanula latiloba alba A bell-flower seen at its best in partial shade. 1.2m × 30cm/4 × 1ft

◆ *Handsome evergreen basal leaves are a winter bonus.*

Phlox divaricata 'May Breeze' has deliciously scented white flowers in early summer. 30 × 20cm/ 1ft × 8in

◆ *This is a lovely cool-looking plant for shade.*

Lilium regale The regal lily is easily grown, given good drainage and sun. 1.2m × 30cm/4 × 1ft

◆ *This midsummer lily is powerfully scented.*

A beautiful single white **peony**, **'White Wings'**, is the star of this early summer border. It is seen against a background of *Crambe cordifolia* with its haze of tiny gypsophila-like flowers. The use of pale apricot **foxgloves** with white avoids the blandness of an entirely white border. White **aquilegias** and *Viola cornuta alba* mingle to complete a tranquil composition.

5. FILLING THE GAPS IN BORDERS

The inevitable gaps that occur in a border provide an excellent opportunity to introduce something temporary.

ANNUALS *and* BIENNIALS

THESE PLANTS ARE EASILY GROWN FROM SEED and are useful for filling large gaps in new borders. Annuals flower in their first year and biennials in their second. Many will self-seed *in situ* and are invaluable for growing in gaps that occur where spring bulbs have died down. Experiment with new ones each year.

Do not pull out lunaria, nigella or opium poppies after flowering, they make attractive seed-heads.

Sweet William and love-in-a-mist are good cut flowers as are annual gypsophila and cornflowers.

Gilia capitata An unusual, dainty annual toning well with delphiniums which flower at the same time. ○, 45 × 20cm/1½ft × 8in

These delicate, slender, annual **Shirley poppies** bloom in midsummer. They have developed from the red field poppy, *Papaver rhoeas*. Allow to self-seed for next year.

◆ Papaver somniferum, *the opium poppy, a larger sturdier poppy, has superb seed-heads.*

Nicotiana langsdorffii A green-flowered tobacco plant with a long, narrow, bell-shaped flower. 1m × 30cm/3 × 1ft

Nigella damascena ('Love-in-a-mist') Useful for a blue and white planting scheme. Self-seeds discreetly. 45 × 20cm/1½ft × 8in

Cosmos A long-flowering, tall annual. Raise in pots to fill unexpected gaps in the borders. 1m × 60cm/3 × 2ft

Dianthus barbatus An auricula-eyed Sweet William gives an old-fashioned look to early summer borders. ◯, 45 × 30cm/1½ × 1ft

Salvia sclarea var. **turkestanica** A dominant biennial with big hairy leaves and lavender-purple bracts. 75 × 30cm/2½ × 1ft

Myosotis alpestris There are also pink and white forms of the forget-me-not. 30 × 30cm/1 × 1ft

Lunaria annua 'Alba Variegata' This white-flowered, variegated biennial honesty is unusual. 75 × 30cm/2½ × 1ft

Many annuals make sturdier plants if sown in autumn, as they would be in the wild.

Look out for self-sown annuals when you are weeding in spring and avoid the hoe.

Limnanthes douglasii The poached-egg plant is a good front row annual for a sunny spot. 15 × 15cm/ 6 × 6in

Cheiranthus cheiri Grow wallflowers as biennials. Good mixers with all spring bulbs. 45 × 30cm/1½ × 1ft

Calendula officinalis Marigolds are usually orange but paler shades of apricot and cream are available. ◯, 45 × 30cm/ 1½ × 1ft

HALF-HARDY PERENNIALS

Pelargonium 'Velvet Duet'
One of the little pelargoniums of the Angel group, with flowers like violas. They make charming gap-fillers. ○, 20 × 20cm/ 8 × 8in

Argyranthemum 'Vancouver' Paris daisies or marguerites have pink, white or yellow, single or double daisies in abundance. ○, 1 × 1m/ 3 × 3ft

Osteospermum 'Buttermilk'
Cool pale yellow petals fading towards the dark centre are unusual. ○, 60 × 30cm/2 × 1ft

◆ *Remove flowers as they die to encourage more.*

Arctotis × hybrida 'Apricot'
Red, white and yellow African daisies are good for 'hot' summer beds. ○, 45 × 30cm/1½ × 1ft

Use pelargoniums (commonly known as geraniums) in shades that are sympathetic to their bed-fellows.

Sphaeralcea munroana makes a mat of foliage covered in flowers all summer. *S. fendleri* is a paler pink. ○, 30cm × 1m/1 × 3ft

THESE PLANTS MAKE A VALUABLE CONTRIBUTION to the summer border, flowering with abundance all season long. They are not winter-hardy so need to be propagated from cuttings every year in late summer and over-wintered in a frost-free greenhouse. Alternatively the plants may be dug up, re-potted and given similar protection.

Cosmos atrosanguineus A curiosity: dark reddish-brown flowers smelling of chocolate. ○, 60 × 45cm/ 2 × 1½ft

Heliotropium peruvianum Plant this beside a seat on the terrace where its scent can be appreciated. 60 × 60cm/2 × 2ft

Solanum rantonnetii makes a sizeable free-flowering shrub in one year from cuttings. ○, 1.5 × 1.2m/ 5 × 4ft

◆ *This looks best in a border against a wall.*

Felicia amelloides A wonderful clear blue, yellow-centred daisy. ○, 45 × 45cm/1½ × 1½ft

BULBS *and* TUBERS

BULBS ADD AN ELEMENT OF SURPRISE IN A BORDER: they appear when we have forgotten that we have planted them! Hardy bulbs such as daffodils are left in the soil and multiply to make big clumps. Tender subjects such as dahlias and gladioli will need to be lifted in autumn and given winter protection.

Tulipa **'Purissima'** Perfect with yellow polyanthus and good dark green foliage. ○, 40 × 20cm/16 × 8in

Narcissus **'Rip van Winkle'** A tough little double daffodil, perfect for a raised bed. It multiplies rapidly. 15 × 15cm/6 × 6in

Gladiolus byzantinus An early gladiolus that can be left in the ground. The later, more flamboyant grandiflorus and primulinus gladioli are not hardy. ○, 60 × 15cm/2ft × 6in

Order your bulbs early in the season to ensure that you get those you want.

Allium christophii Huge spectacular flower heads. Try to place a low plant in front to disguise the allium foliage which always becomes untidy. ○, 45 × 20cm/1½ft × 8in

◆ *The seed-heads dry perfectly and are much sought after by flower arrangers.*

Fritillaria imperialis A
stately spring bulb for
good well-drained soil in
sun or partial shade.
Crown imperials have a
ring of orange, red or
yellow flowers on tall leafy
stems, crowned with a tuft
of leaves. The bulbs
should be planted on their
sides with some coarse
sand. 1.5m × 30cm/5 × 1ft

Fritillaria persica A
sophisticated fritillary
with a fascinating grape-
like bloom on its leaves
and its purple-black
flowers. A challenge to
grow in rich, well-
drained soil in sun. ○,
75 × 30cm/2½ × 1ft

CLIMBERS

Eccremocarpus scaber A long succession of red, yellow or orange flowers for full sun. Easy to grow from seed which is produced in abundance. 3m/10ft

The sweet pea, *Lathyrus odoratus*, is an excellent annual climber to grow on a bamboo wig-wam.

Canary creeper (*Tropaeolum peregrinum*) is a yellow flowered, fast-growing annual climber with attractive leaves.

Clematis texensis hybrids, with their tulip-shaped flowers, are ideal to grow through winter heathers.

Clematis alpina **'Pamela Jackman'** is seen here climbing through the new variegated leaves of *Sambucus nigra* 'Marginata'. No regular pruning is required but it may be cut back immediately after flowering. 2m/6ft

◆ Clematis macropetala *is similar but has semi-double flowers. Pink and white forms of both available.*

Humulus lupulus 'Aureus' A wonderful, yellow-leaved form of hop making vigorous sprawling annual growth. In a small garden confine it to a pole. 4m/13ft

CLIMBING PLANTS are generally grown on a wall or fence at the back of the border or up a pole or obelisk to add height. Less formally they can be used to scramble into established shrubs or allowed to sprawl forwards to cover the dying foliage of earlier flowers.

Tropaeolum speciosum **(Flame creeper)** Often seen adorning yew hedges and favouring cool, moist, acid soils. 3m/10ft

Clematis × durandii has a very long flowering season. Lovely scrambling through *Brachyglottis* 'Sunshine'. 1.5 × 1.5m/5 × 5ft

Lathyrus rotundifolius The Persian everlasting pea has early summer flowers of an unusual shade of soft brick red. 2m/6ft

◆ *Unfortunately this decorative pea has no perfume.*

This very formal border alongside a shady path uses repetition of identically planted urns to achieve unity. *Hedera helix* **'Parsley Crested'** is the ivy used. Spilling across the path are *Hosta* **'Thomas Hogg'** and *Alchemilla mollis*. The ivy will look good at all seasons but will be the dominant feature in winter when the herbaceous plants are dormant.

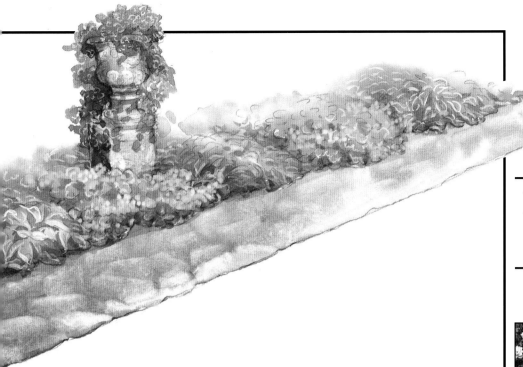

UNEXPECTED GAPS IN BORDERS can be filled with plants kept in reserve in pots: lilies and hostas are excellent for this purpose. The pots give added height and importance to the plants. In a formal setting large terracotta pots will reinforce the formality and can be replanted seasonally.

A shallow pot, planted with silver saxifrages, has been raised on a plinth to give it more importance.

The lilies in this border are growing in a large pot. When they have finished flowering they can be replaced by a later flowering lily.

◆ *It is important to remember to water plants in pots used in borders.*